GOLD PASSAGE

Gold Passage

Poems by Iris Jamahl Dunkle

Winner of the 2012 Trio Award

Copyright © Iris Jamahl Dunkle 2013

No part of this book may be used or performed without written consent from the author, if living, except for critical articles or reviews.

Dunkle, Iris Jamahl.
1ˢᵗ edition.

ISBN: 978-0-9855292-0-8
Library of Congress Control Number: 2012954358

Interior Layout by Lea C. Deschenes
Cover Design by Dorinda Wegener
Cover Art by Martha Wade
Editing by Tayve Neese and Lisa Sisler

Printed in Tennessee, USA
Trio House Press, Inc.
Fernandina Beach, FL
Ponte Vedra Beach, FL

To contact the author, send an email to books@TrioHousePress.com

For Tortuga, Jackson, and Maxwell.

GOLD PASSAGE

HOME – MADE

13	Dinosaur
14	Door Poem Between the Self and the Heart
15	California
16	The Conversation a Little Girl has with Herself is the Size of an Apple
17	The Naming
18	What Falls from the Sky
20	Autopsy of a Day
21	Sebastopol
23	After Elegy
25	Bobcat
26	Hawk, Fire
27	Worlds are Being Told like Beads
28	Between the Word and the Sense
30	Ballad of Air
31	Cormorant

WATER ROOT

35	Carp
36	Photography Lesson: Point Reyes
37	Inside/Out
38	Desire, Please Burn Off
39	The Woman at the River's Edge

40	The View from Mercer Hospital, Pittsburgh, PA
41	At Hellig Hooge
42	Often I Return to a River
43	Body's Code
44	Fear: the After-Thirst Diving in
45	She was Seen Walking Naked into the Trees
46	Sonoma
47	Bodega Bay
48	Risk of Oak, Freestone CA
49	Inheritance

MOTHER TREE

53	The Distance Between
56	Thanksgiving
58	Strange Animal
59	To the Cherry Blossoms at Prospect Park
60	Moth and Rust
61	We Two Were Sisters of a Strange, Isolated Little Family
63	Gold Passage
64	Our Flesh, Delivered by Ghosts
65	Her Voice Grabbed Me So Hard I Almost Remembered Who I Was
66	The Dress
67	Sister
68	Cave Redux
70	Witness
71	Cartography of Home

72	What We Found Here
73	Trick of Sound
74	Gift

HOME-MADE

"*Home-made, home-made! But aren't we all?*"
—ELIZABETH BISHOP, "Crusoe in England"

"*I don't know who made the ground;
it was here when I was born.*"
—TOM SMITH

Dinosaur

You can feel the sadness of the large head
that floats like a planet in the museum,

the metronome of feet shuffling past
a little sun powdering the lifted dust   and its *haloed*.

*Weeks,   years,   knees
red-raw in the dug dirt.*

A scientist dug you free and spelt you out for your new skin.

Now the dinosaur contains what we imagined:
a life that's visible we can reconstruct,

and all these people shuffling past
Faith, or what church do you believe in.

What's behind the glass behind the skin of this life as we pass

*I am an alphabet of bones,
my own telling.*

Door Poem Between the Self and the Heart

There is a great expanse of blue, and somewhere
on that horizon is a great gift: *a mite in the eye, a begin again.*

This is *on the threshold of*   a door poem,
which moans   *as old wood does.*

This close, I can see the whirls of its intricate grains—
I can feel the hard stand   *that old guard*
of its cells   *those little soldiers*   against me—

But time, and the blue cloak that continually passes
above our heads, was on my side.

I wasn't some drunken girl begging
on the sandpaper pavement for *it*
or redemption.
It was me I was talking to, after all,
and what existed on the other side of that door
was, well, unknowable.

That's when it happened: I looked up.
I pulled the two scythe moons of my eyes
up to meet whatever gods and names
the paint-by-number sky could dream,

and I bloomed like a god-damned hyacinth:

constellations of my skin,
nebulous clouds of my mind,
the dark, brooding unknown,

aligned, until that door wasn't anything more than a door.

California

I want to tear off my skin and give it back to God.

I spent my childhood longing for trains and a way
to get back from—

Now, the whole city swells and whimpers on its haunches,
afraid of its own intentions.

It is difficult to distinguish history in all this chatter.

But, springs arrives, and even the sleepy-eyed hills
are loosening their golden pelts
like overgrown elephant seals.

Sit up! *the tiny hands of spring*
the tiny hands of rain

are untying, are trying to talk

and life, life!
is awakening again
like a good dog.

Let the animals sleep and the day repair itself.

We'll trace their shapes in the sky at night.

God: here's the landscape I'm born to—

Let me tell it.

The Conversation a Little Girl has with Herself is the Size of an Apple

When the little girl woke she discovered
she was wearing an apron all covered

in dirt, but *clean slate* the apple was
gone. All she had left of it was the space
it once contained. So she swallowed the space,
let the tiny balloon rise to her head,

the apple's color filling her cheeks: *red!*
red! I said, the conversation, I said,
a little girl has herself: an apple.

The Naming

> *"'Listen Red Comb,' said the donkey; 'would you like to run away with us? We are going to Bremen, and you will find something better there than to be made into soup; you have a fine voice and if we all play together it will have a good effect.'"*
> —from *The Bremen Town Musicians*

Mt. Tam held my name on its tongue like a secret.
My father, my mother, young, pouring down from it, saw,
the wild irises yawn like purple lions:
wild pocks on the mountain's blue arched back.

I was named still floating brackish in the belly jar.

Mountain, Mountain, O where to begin.
Now you turn like the corner,
a mite in my eye   my   nemesis
my begin   again.

I was lucky, my mountain, born with you already under my
    bare blue feet.

When I woke up miles away from my birth
I was more tired than when I had begun.
I didn't recognize my own face, the face of a lion
looking back from the mirror.

Will you accept this false history I've left of you for a clean slate?

I'm ready to become more then my name.

What Falls from the Sky

1

When my brother and I flew the kite
we thought it was an experiment in weather.
Each of us fought to follow the cord out
and up, giving more line, until finally
we had to tie it to the farthest corner
of the barbed wire fence. That night, the storm claimed it.

At school, when we were given balloons,
we were told to tie messages to their strings—let them go,
in hopes that when they fell
from the sky, someone would find our blessings.

My brother and I already knew
no one would find them—
love is what lifts up and leaves.

2

I was convinced my mother was dying.
She stood so often at the silver sink, washing dishes,
her hands were pink and raw. Sometimes,
she'd even wash my hair in it   *silver*
her hair she painted red
because only children should contain their age.

When she stayed in bed for a week
part of me remained by her bedside, praying,
the other part (my father) had already left.

3

I don't remember it landing like a miracle
in the backyard,
men in the fields gathering yards and yards
of the balloon's silk shining cloth
in their out-stretched arms.

Out from the basket spilled
a husband, a wife, still dressed for their wedding
as if they had just fallen off a cake.

All afternoon, the house shifted with their weight
as their laughter colored the dark house yellow.

After they left, I found their rings at the sink—
two gold bands shining in the soap dish.

4

The trick of memory is—it fills itself out:

My father has returned.
It is raining.
How small he looks standing
like a wet bird
in the gape of the open door.
He smiles
at my brother, at me,
at my mother lingering behind us.
He's holding flowers
as if he's brought spring itself.
And the curtain falls over the whole house.

It doesn't lift for years.

Autopsy of a Day

There is water near the celebration,
a rocky beach, pebbles the size of peas.

In the photograph I'll find after, he stands slightly askew,
his arm looped around me. We are the same height,
bound by history and this second—
then he's gone, weaving back into the laughter,
into the strange, moving bodies.

The sun is letting go—when I walk out
the long dock away from the beach and look back:
a small fire shaves sparks into the grey dusk,
a life grows like a long shadow toward night,

and I feel like I am in a boat pushing
away   out to the sense of sea.

SEBASTOPOL

It's hard won fitness climbing
the ashen road that carries you up
the "Three Sisters" by bike.
Three ever steeper climbs—hot,
exposed—until the summit.
At the top, the air is cool
beneath thick-knuckled trees.

Today, at the peak all is bare.
The trees split like boxed bodies in a magic trick.

Many fields have been cleared.
Apples for grapes. The new farmers say: Apples
are yesterday—as they till the earth for a new crop.
The old, who for generations have trimmed
the delicate limbs of the Gravenstein,
are now red-faced and gnarled as their heirloom trees.

At the top, the ridge is a permeable line
between green hills that roll to the sea
and the patchwork of farmed valley that leads to town.
What is good/bad is brackish as history:
a two-day stand-off between two men,
one inside the general store, the other
pacing the street. Nothing could come between.
Crowds gathered murmuring,
it's like the battle of Sebastopol,
and the name stuck. After the naming, what happened?
Someone must have stepped outside
or someone must have stepped inside—
that much isn't remembered.

I crest at the top—this time without stopping,
look out at the ridge dividing sea from town,
push the pedal down, into the descent,
into the rush and risk of air.

After Elegy

for Will Roberts

\<Body\>
\<Sunday 1\>
   The sun spills into playground.
   We sit on porch-swing, watch
   the children play. Sound of pea-gravel,
   and swing's motion—voice stuttering
   already from stroke as he describes
   the history of good apple trees:
   reliance, hard-wood, not prone to
   rot, the promise and scent of fruit.

                                               \</Sunday 1\>

\<Sunday 2\>

   He greets chaos eye-to-eye, hand out-stretched, palm
   to welcoming palm. Chorals already powdering the
   cacophonous space behind him.

                                               \</Sunday 2\>

\<Sunday 3\>

   If   (the girl hears hospice)
      then she packs a basket filled with all that heals:
      a salve for the heart, sliced crisp apples, words cool as
      a sunlit creek
 else
      the girl smiles and follows the children out through
      the bright door instead
      sweeping the word under the carpet with the dust.

                                             \</Sunday 3\>

<Sunday 4>

    print "Orchards, or what remains"
    print "after the fire"
    print "after the bright vision of loss"
    print "cool fog lulls"
    print "what will bulb"
    print "on the remaining limbs"

Children still weaving
through blackened trees
infecting the air
with muscle and joy.

                                          </Sunday 4>

</Body>

Bobcat

Here on my doorstep,
cricket song and frog swell.
By now, the bobcat
I'd spotted in the front yard
is deep in the woods—
his freedom full and risen as a moon.

My matter is never freed
from urban tongue and lure.
I pace my house, plot escape,
jump at whistles of tea kettles,
the screams of time's alarms
while the bobcat freely looms
in memory. Overhead,
planes fly courses, leave
long contrails that linger,
dissolve, but stay.

Hawk, Fire

From this height fire loses its fear,
becomes velvet pouring over the landscape.

We live between two worlds:
one seen from 10,000 feet, and another seen at ground level,

a spot on the map between two ancient pine trees
where hawks train their young to fly—
one sharp point to another—*it's all air,*
and us, dumb, beneath.

The green hills that surround
are pocked with old, arthritic oaks.
So much rain this year, the roots,
what's underneath, might rot,
pushing up from their dark inheritance.

My story is always pushing up
while my love stays low to the ground, rooted.

When the fire raged up the hill toward the house it was
no longer a river of rubies seen from 10,000 feet.
It was ravenous—
an open mouth,
a heart turned inside out.

And after, what can grow?
What stories have been awakened like tiny phoenixes
gathering strength, rising, flapping their ashen wings
under the hawk's watch?

Worlds are Being Told like Beads

Glass touch, finger to finger—
blue light dusting the children,
projecting the film strips of their futures
onto the constellations of their skin.

The red fox wanders into the room
like luck,
like the unimaginable,

and the white moths of darkness flit and banter the windows.
Each child stands. One amongst the others.
Their small bodies foretold, but un-telling.

The fox, only a red vision.
When he leaves. When the children close their eyes:

they see black, calm water,
new moon spilling a pearl passage forward into now.

Between the Word and the Sense

1

In German, *ruhig* means peace: a place, carved out
orb of light, belly of a firefly, not built, but comes soothing, pelt-like
skin of Madrone that peels and peels towards smooth.

To find *ruhig* you must travel a long distance.
You must have tensed and clenched and winced and shied.
Ruhig is the space the body can make—deep, submerged
in a warm sea or under an avalanche of doubt—
a trick of breath and life.

2

In the 7-11 parking lot the car next to mine opens like a cinema. Man, dirty tank top, slaps skinny woman with stringy brown hair across the face. His anger is *Vesuvial,* covering the world in red velvet fire, leaving only a blanket of ash and the possibility of later archeology: rooms, hidden and sealed, left intact. The child is in the backseat, in pajamas at noon.

I'm three feet away, caged in metal but thinking *sweet, silent Doppelgänger, I know you, I know you.*

The celluloid stretched out reads: *don't judge*. Your car door swings wide open into (*Say it!*) the word I want to give that child is bigger than my whole fleshy body.

3

The artist is learning disaster—flown, all expenses paid, to descend into the sealed rooms of Pompeii. What she finds will be painted in someone else's dining room.

4

Like golden elephant seal pelts, the hills spill to the road,
soothing back the asphalt as the trees spindle the sky just high enough to pass me through.

This road leads to home, to dinner, to a chance at grace:
two sets of sticky hands,
tiny, electric wire bodies,
eyes that can't yet close long enough.

And in our waning stillness, we'll carve that cavity between us—

Ballad of Air

Birds weave lines
between these towns—
white crane, blue heron,
bodies too large to rise,
risk wobbling
each careful stoke of wing.

        Somewhere in the south,
        there is a city made only of words:
        where monkeys roar like lions
        then sleep; where fear s-weaves
        and slithers at our feet.
        Ink follows each heavy footstep,
        each careful movement of the tongue and jaw.
        Even the vines will spell us out—

Air is the want of weight,
want of the earth's stay,
what fire yearns to become
when ashes rise
like delicate moths.
Let them satiate here—in this.
Let them touch to find
each word breathlessly
leaving our mouths.

Cormorant

Morning, and I walk past the man-made lake
where the bird gulls for light—I am just birthed
from Thor's flash and spite— *the bright white thorn of
knobbed sleep and the throb of light a risk of
life*   I feel important—survived
a part of the whole force that pulses past

but the dumb sea bird doesn't stir, just stays
erect as a piece of the alphabet
waiting to burn clean its wings.

*under a blue-cloud-bespeckled sky
under the blue domed egg*

who wouldn't expect flight?

How small am I.

WATER ROOT

"We came into the world at the edge of a stream."
—JULIANA SPAHR, "Gentle Now, Don't Add to Heartache"

Carp

The woman watches the carp swim as if they were her pets behind the houseboat. They weave behind in the small, still wake—watching the woman watch them. She is dreaming of Christmas in Czechoslovakia. The slurp and slop from the upstairs tub. The oversized carp circling, searching for an escape: the plop and sink of the coppery coins. The taste. But here, in this land, the surprised river is blooming colors from the dye factory and, like a fairytale, the carp magically transform back into their true states: her two stout children. The girl is pale and blue, the boy, red. It is the man who pulls them out of the wake, washes the dye from their skin as they flop on the deck. The woman watches from her wooden chair as the children transform again: pale, white and delicate as porcelain.

Photography Lesson: Point Reyes

My father teaches me landscape
here, where the land itself cannot decide
to which age it raises its stiff thumb.

I have a decision to make—
a few names to throw into the ocean.

We walk up the bare beach.
We look through a machine.
He says *don't forget
you are looking through a machine.*

Your emotions will ruin it.

The hills beyond are almost bald—
a lone raven marks in an arc their curve
then lands still in a nest of waves.

Ravens, he says, *will never appear in pairs.*

I push the shutter down
let the machine realize
what I have learned
as something scares the bird to flight.

Why must stories overlap? I ask
but my father is already walking away—
the machine ticking faster
than waves can count.

Inside/Out

I used to think it shy, my old heart,
some shade-hidden salamander
making music, nudging underwater rocks
beneath rotten leaves,
clouds of sediment blossoming up.

But these days, it's risen—
boiled up—so to speak.

Rock arteries stuck
with grey nets of leaves' skeletons;
flat, moss-covered rock
water rushing through fingers toward
a life carved by unpredictable weather.

Flash forward to now:

The same creek. The same damn heart.
My children's small bodies splashing
red and yellow rain boots
their bodies bent
their fingers cleaning the same limestone arteries
as I sit, watch water wearing the banks.

Desire, Please Burn Off

Stitched into the mountain's side are switchbacks.
What is too steep to come down in winter—
is climbable now: rock by slipping rock.

    Behind the mountain, moonlight floods the lake—wooing.

Thick forests of aspen tremor in wind's tenor.
With luck you'll find an arborglyph amongst them:
faces carved into the skin of a thin,
quivering tree. Love or self is like that.

        Swallowed by the murmurous static of aspen leaves.

Climb up and up. Reach trail head. Birds who once
stitched fear to earth lifted to flight. Creek, snow melt,
boulders, fist-sized pebbles, nest of sticks catch

only the motion of—

           [desire, please burn off]

Where is the path of mercy you promised?

The Woman at the River's Edge

for L.N. and M.P.

In the myth, the hands were not placed on the table before they were cut off. They were eaten slowly. Gnawed, by time, by the animals who had been standing on her back. It was a bird-less dawn when she awoke and noticed their absence. The cool of the sheets rubbed against her raw wounds. By then, there was no one to blame. The animals had all climbed down and taken roost in the eaves. So, to see another part of herself removed, it wasn't surprising. Felt natural. The water that pulls past the house tangles the weeds and troubles the rocks, but even it eddies. Here she was. Morning. Crisp new sheets. She should be thinking: *the possibility of day.* But the mind swells with the storm, carries what's lost on its deep current. Throbs.

The View from Mercer Hospital, Pittsburgh, PA

for Ken

Tantalus sits eleven stories up
pressed in glass—a cool eye skating the cool
river that interrupts in ice below.
He is a man between—a butterfly
observed on pins: his own imprisoned face
reflecting back at him—a stranger, thin and
out of place. A gray man in a gray place.
Who wouldn't believe escape? That just
one bright apple, crisp to the lips, wet to
the touch, might be permitted. But, the tongue
recoils. The stomach sulks. The walls move in
until he no longer sees his own face—
just the cool, gray, river below
the city, forever carried on its back.

At Hellig Hooge

From the ferry in, tiny islands rise defiant from the slack sea.
Three or four houses stand held together by paths.
Not a tree in site. Inside, the hearth is stamped in cool blue tile.
A small sign advertises that a king visited here once, stayed overnight.

The island has no engines, only the thick coils of calf and thighs—

fear puncture, fear growing thick,
fear bicycle spokes,
fear thick buttered bakes of mushrooms and cream
fear a storm, a sea that can swallow everything.

History is a hungry sea.
The shore here seeps—you won't notice years have passed.

We are drawn to the church because we heard singing.

Pews of the church
fenced like tiny wooden boats.
Sea frothed like boiled over tea covered the ancient graveyard

                           headstones
             like crooked teeth.
             The dead can swim here   *are risen*

Often I Return to a River

It is as if the river is malleable, editable,
where shadowed depths kick up soot
that first clouds, then slowly reveals, an altered
universe where narratives overlap.

Beneath the surface, a net of sunlight
and fish: tiger shark, steelhead, shrimp. Silt fills
the slough, over a long crawl of years.
To find what is river, history, one

must dredge it out—sea birds lift, disturbed
by a pontoon floated down to
San Pablo Bay. Here, I pass my father—
his long hair a rope down his browned, thin back

as he constructs a floating house, a life.
Me, I'm traveling back up—disturbing
what's left of the banks. Water distorts our
lives. Mine, a life he set me adrift upon, I'll

continually revise. Cool water, thick
with brackish history, re-writeable
by the muscular action of bodies.

What crane will see us passing and rise
prophetic, until camouflaged by clouds?

Body's Code

\<open\> in the heart's language
dawn unlocks its gray jaw
silver pouring
upon the river's quivering skin \</open\>
\<closed\> the body fumbles \</closed\>
\<truth\> *learning through repetition* \</truth\>

the dawn breaks
the dawn breaks again
the body fumbles
the body is breakable

if the body wakes
then the dawn will swell silver and quiver on the river's open scar.

if this body is breakable
then
               on waking *stand*
               on sleeping *let go*
a raw wound
an unwinding of skeins and skeins of intricate threads:

    the violet soaked wool of life's frail regality

\<chance\> life quivers like that river caught
in sun's dying or waking light \</chance\>

if I throw a stone
then a world like a mouth will open up in the river's tumbling song.

Fear: the After-Thirst Diving in

The white barked trees lean into wind's tenor
on lake's shore.   To dive in. To break the calm.

Body as conduit into clouded
depths of rocks and soot.   Let go the balloon

of air that's held you up.   We are untouched
tapestries of tissues falling beneath

blue surface of forget. Cold shock of stories
whisper into arms, legs. Thrust of kick. Arm

arrows. Arm arrows again. Mind succumbs.
Something underground that doesn't speak, grows.

What is the glamour of flesh in all this ache and want?

She was Seen Walking Naked into the Trees

The sound of her toes nudging rocks.

The sound of rocks against rocks.

The stone sisters that surround her like sleeping giants.

Beneath the surface the body lifts and gathers light.

There are islands to be found in shadows, even beneath the surface.

Out beyond—desire is limitless as a lake.

Sonoma

History carves spoon-like,
the push and pull of creek's water
on limestone bed:
change that breathes.

With a pocket compass and a good eye,
a few paces became a town square:
rows of open-eyed houses staring
toward a broad avenue reaching to the sea.

Time will chip and pick at each façade
and sea will comb and comb
the grey wool of memory
until it is freed of knots.

Bodega Bay

1

My history is half-dipped in waters too cold to swim,
but spot the imaginary buoy marking red, lit with risk,

and I'm still game minded: Simon says *take three strokes forward.*
However many strokes I take from shore, I come back more

                                                [elastic]

2

Here, along the scar of coast, we like to spin wool,
yarns grey but backlit by the inevitable pink of dawn.

Hoards of black birds descend in an ellipse
only to rest between telephone poles,

markers of who survived to tell—a few houses:
a school, a church, like busted pickets on a sea-stained fence.

What seeps in covers the bright golden pelts of hills
in reverberating songs   [piercing calls of hawks]

3

O! Sonora!
In your swollen wooden belly,
the rot of wood six months at sea,
life looked close in a glass,   [breath fogging the mirror]

white canvas sails stretched wide and spinning clouds,
bridging fog from the brackish cold below.

Shore-bound, open abalone shells already abandoned for their meat
reflect sorrow onto the same tinted clouds.
Four cannons were dragged, rocky sand,   [cast iron]
the weight still sinking in.

Risk of Oak, Freestone CA

Small stop on the North Pacific Coast Railroad expands, contracts, becomes a town.

Stories rustle like dead leaves, then lift up, revealing a few moments backlit by light,

like the day she walked into town beneath the tall oaks and mist swallowed her footsteps.

Crack sharp as thunder. Then, the gnarled oak, older than this stone quarry town, uprooted,

fell. Dirt raining in an arc. Her story, wedded to this place, these stones, continued

to walk on the hissing pavement. Emptiness of stones taken, the weight of those that remain.

While her moment gathers wind, spells passage to the other, unexpected life.

Inheritance

The woman on the shore wants a map
to transform the water back
into the city it once was.
All day the trees will push
shade out toward the birds.

A shadow can only be what it reflects upon.
She thinks about hers
and the waves, the watery
passage that pushes at her form.

She wishes for a wooden boat, a clear day free of wind
to follow the fingers
of trees, to float above the stillborn
houses that blink up like dioramas.
She imagines the blossom of torn curtains.
A table still set and waiting.
The story of home.

But she doesn't have boat, or a map,
just a patchwork of stories sewn thick
into her ear, and her dark
shadow growing towards the center
of the lake.

MOTHER TREE

"Because it is my country
And I speak to it of itself
And sing of it with my own voice"
—AMY LOWELL, "Lilacs"

The Distance Between

1

Grateful for the tree, not just what's air-bound:

>*oak trunk thick enough to thwart cannon balls*
>*black bark, dark tributaries opening*
>*arthritically toward sky*

                                                          but also what's

beneath soil's vinculum:

                                                          uncharted roots

>*blind animals pushing toward light, toward*
>*idea of water—belief it will be found.*

2

August 19, 2010

Dear 206 Million Gallons of Oil—

The freeway ashes golden valley like a cross
carelessly smudged on our foreheads. Drive. Drive.

Some days I log 200 – 300 miles. A long commute
to work and back. Kids to soccer in minivan.

Can't you see there is no bus, no feet to
carry the weight of this: *No other way.*

Loom, stalk us like the Blob. Even when radios stop slopping
their electronic tongues.

How you bloom and cloud the sea. Weeks pour into
months. It's not your motion we are fighting.

In you I bloom too —

what have you dredged up from the deep?

3

When I speak about the oil spill I am also speaking about the cut redwood trees on Exit 116 of Highway 101. How they jut like decapitated bodies in the low fog.

I am speaking of the bright language of orange poppies. State flower. My children's questions about whether or not they are allowed to pick those bright, oily petals.

About the earnings report and how we will craft the message to meet the market's expectations. Then later, re-craft it to meet employee expectations.

Bumper to bumper traffic. Stuck. Looking at burnt hills. Looking through closed windows into grimacing faces. How far away my children's voices sound on a static filled cell phone call.

How sun cuts, has sharpened. How even the oaks bend away from its want.

I'm thinking about how to make a story that will broadcast this distance:

> *There was once a sea*
> *that blossomed oil*
> *until the sea became sick*
> *until we looked into it*
> *and saw ourselves.*

Thanksgiving

A year ago today, the sun shone bright in the city.
Walking home from the dry cleaners I felt
the shadow flit behind me, moth-like,
then suddenly, in front of me—
dead eyes, hood up, gun drawn. My red, brick home
just steps away, was unreachable. World
overexposed. Screams scissoring the air.

                After,
the bruises. The found empty purse.
The neighborhood hedged by threat. Empty
echoes of shots fired in dumpsters. Squad cars
circling the block. Anger, patrolling us
like a rabid dog. And so we left, wandered
far as we could away from the city.

Now, I'm waiting for a tide of forgiveness
to wash in, even here, where the hills roll
green and smooth to the sea. Where the air is
thick with memory, salt, and fog.

A rafter of wild turkeys mill
on the sun-drenched field—safely wild,
even today. I toss stale bread.
They take the charity, scatter
to the woods without fear or regard.

Don't we all contain these two
interwoven stories—divided by chance—
the good dog curled by
the fire, the wild, fleeing animal?

One half of me is still running, clutching my old life,
that risk — into the unknown, while the other is
here, domesticated and safe,
fattening the wild turkeys—

before we sit down at the table, give thanks, and eat.

Strange Animal

After the rain
a Canada goose
found itself islanded
on our tiny field
through a break in the trees.

All day her distress
broadcast across
the entire valley

until I became her echo
writing down
her ever tangling loops
of failed ascent.

To the Cherry Blossoms at Prospect Park

My body reclines, reads
their delicate snow,
as sunlight fans through
their thin, dark silhouettes.

After so many seasons
I have found other trees:
Gravenstein apples, Bosch pears, quince
whose blossoms now explode
under threat of rain
like pink fists pushing toward light.

Come fall's winds and winter's crowding
their tart fruit will be there for the taking
now I harvest—
now I feed many, hungry mouths.

Moth and Rust

What the astronauts must see
when they orbit the earth—
blue-black velvet press of silence,
the distant ache for a small blue bead.
How comforting to be tethered only
to the command voice of the control room.

Here, on the lull and lumber of the earth,
plates scrape. Born on a fault. Taught helplessly,
to tuck and cover beneath desks too small,
to expect the earth's insatiable
mouth to swallow up us and all we love.

Truth is, death will not be convenient or scheduled.
Life will not be a shedding—
an unwinding towards center or clear command.
Love's fierce heart will stoke like a coal

without reflection. What the moth eats, what
time rusts, will float away—until remains
only the risk of love, blue, and moving away.

We Two Were Sisters of a Strange, Isolated Little Family

"Ah, me! I wish I could have talked to Sappho,
Surprised her reticences by flinging mine
Into the wind."
—"The Sisters," Amy Lowell

1

Growing up I passed Indian Rock in a yellow
school bus on the snake and slide of highway.
The story goes: two lovers, despite their warring tribes,
sprang from the little pedestal at the
top into love or death or the rocky
river below. In every town there seems
to be a story gifted between generations, some Leucadian leap
to cure the shame of loving wrong.

2

Little girls grow up learning want—a tether
between two ballooned souls—husband,
wife. When he boils up
her world is fogged. His/Her world,
simple as a sea cliff, a five-story rock.
But the husband/the wife see only his/her own reflection
in the water below. And the tether is bogged
down by the weight of the low-fog.
Over the years, love appears like fireflies—
known, but always a surprise.

3

But motherhood consumes the heart.
Wrong, says society, or *this is
a mother*, or *this is the right amount
of cord to the heart.* As her self burns to a dull flame.

She has become the cool water transparent to her depths
or muddied with the storm of – *here, is my*

heart. It's a tight walk between what's left of self
and the far shore.

4

Now, I stand at the drop— push and shove
of love's burden—blur of centuries,
and the simplicity of it floats down
petal soft—we sit on the dew-lit lawn—
the bells of our children's voices a blur
with all the orchestras of spring. It weaves
a thick rope to our hearts until we are
tethered, willingly. I love my son.
I say to Sappho as she smiles at me.

> *It's a good leap. She says.*

And we laugh as the day,
that consuming fire,
swallows us up.

Gold Passage

for Lotta Crabtree and Lola Montez

1

In Grass Valley, the child star who tap-danced
on an anvil at miners' camps was taught
the ancient dance tarantella,
a movement once used to trick the body,
bitten by spiders, into health.

Her teacher, her face, granite-edged,
displayed on the stage in her dark saloon
how one can shimmy and turn
the past toward a redemptive light
that only birds can see.

2

What illumines our path forward is what once consumed us—

a projection answered in showers of gold dust,
more than what can fit in a tiny shoe.

3

Today, we push bowls of alms toward the sky. We record
    scales of our notations.

But we forget we are fragments in ascent—
the thick, black-cabled trolley that glides
dangerously close to cliffs confessing
history like lovers in hot, punctuated breath.

At the center of the mountain a cool, undiscovered lake resides.
Chorus of voices whisper beneath water's skin—*you are not alone.*
Dangerous, bruised by indecision.

Dive.

Our Flesh, Delivered by Ghosts

for Deborah Digges

1

The Pomo believe sorrow reflects—
worn smooth and bright as abalone shells.

This morning the granite-veined mountains shouted
into that blue, widening of mind:

exultations or siren-songs, that ripen,
drop, and are left to blett in sparse air.

Even flat-lined on steady footing of valley
floor, memory turns over, rustled by

wind: silver dollar shaped aspen leaves turning
olive green to pale in an instant.

2

At Luther Burbank's Experimental Farm,
the mother tree serves also as witness
reaching fifty grafted arms skyward. Fall,
and long into winter blazing the burden of apples:
Gravenstein, Pink Pearl, Etter's Gold, Rome.

You said *pluck high*.
You said *raise a scaffold toward possibility*.

Leave the sound of scattering shells, this long
season of want.

Her Voice Grabbed Me So Hard I Almost Remembered Who I Was

for Sarah Ballard Smith
(Last Native Speaker of the Bodega Miwok Language)

Her voice is reel-to-reel crackling, earthbound, but all air.
Her voice reflects back like the cool, pearled shells of abalone.
Her voice stitched stories out of lightning and rain clouds.
Her voice collected the rains for fear of drought.
Her voice was combed free of the trouble it must have contained.

Her voice could gather salt from the sea, leech acorns
    and smooth clamshells into tiny, white beads.
Her voice was annotated with this currency.
Her voice skimmed the cool, shallow depths of Bodega Bay.
Her voice, quick as a baby tiger shark, darting from the sway
    of kelp leaf to kelp leaf.
Her voice contains the tiny blue stars of forget-me-nots
    and the nervous beauty of quails.
Her voice still lingers in the grey combed clouds that stretch
    across the too, blue sky above the sea.

The Dress

The lemon-yellow dress hangs in the room
that curves like a nautilus. He says, *I've made this dress for you*.
Paris. Green folding chairs freckling the weave of tan, gravel paths.
Time has rolled us around to this moment—

curving like a nautilus. He says, *I've made this dress for you*.
She stands like Aphrodite, naked in the open room,
time has rolled us around to this moment—
the dress falling over her body like light, or air.

She stands like Aphrodite, naked in the open room,
sky darkens as we heave up the slope to Stein's grave.
Dress falling over her body like light, or air.
The Polaroid speaks of contrast—

sky darkens as we heave up the slope toward Stein's grave.
You can see the joy rising like the text of a lost manuscript
in the Polaroid that speaks of contrast—
later, we will leave questions like stones.

You can see the joy rising like the text of a lost manuscript.
After, the wind will carry us like seeds—
where we will sift through a pile of stones,
and bloom into bright sycamores—

I must have been carried by the wind
to have landed so far away here.
Planted, yet still blooming, a bright scarred sycamore.
But, you remain there, unattested as joy.

Paris. Green folding chairs freckling the weave of tan gravel paths.
The nautilus still turns between us—
and always at its center stands
the lemon-yellow dress.

Sister

Helen, I too have been a rag doll—button eyes, sawdust face
blow a breath   and my story   comes apart—
multiplicity—it's what we're made of.

Not chiseled, white marble, blue veins.
Your mind is a labyrinth   we continually   walk into—

The writing on the wall has been fading
turn here!   *get out!*   is muted by decay.

You are sized just right to fit us all.

Your breasts sag after 1000 years.
Your uterus must be a galaxy of stars expanding, blinking on
    and off.

CAVE REDUX

hollow in the earth. hollow out. yield, submit. to mine, mine. open horizontally into

When my bag was packed for the universe, I scrambled down the rough slope, slipped unknowingly inside the sea cave, blinked big-eyed. Surrender was dark and intoxicating. Then the night fell, the stars filling the tiny hole with wide night.

Medusa Looking Out of the Sea Cave

is not grotesque—just misunderstood
green-skinned, golden-eyed anemones
not snakes, crown her sea-salt hair
looking out from all that dark into us
we are of another light
the winged horse springing not
from her blood, but from her lips, O

hollow in the earth. to mine, mine. open horizontally into

but morning found dawn and dawn found hope had stuck those same stars inside. The days washed in and the days washed out. Wet walls gleaming with one-thousand golden eyes. Eyes, growing accustomed to the dark. Sea licking my ankles like comfort.

hollow earth. to mine, mine. open into

The horizon holds a bright line between two shades of blue. Expect rescue I think. But I forget to wish a ship, mutiny, an island born of volcanic ash where a small, yellow orchid might find root in a crevice of the red, pocked cliffs pounded by the sea.

Years pass the earth opens, mine, mine

until I breathe the smell of the sea. It covers me in veils of salt. Until I prefer the gift of dark. The small bodies that cradle my legs. Until my words float out of the cave covered in salt.

Witness

There is some luck involved
the way this land has reared me.
Another apple season follows the last:
Gravenstein to Etta's Gold.

Stories that mumble from the far-off creek
howl muddy loud in a good storm.
Under the ashen road the old North Pacific
Railroad sings to me in sleep: *good daughter—*
a child looking at ruins grows younger.

Dig and dig until all the bones are found.

Cartography of Home

In this landscape certainty lulls like a false lover—

>   hawk's call persists,
>   dawn's bruise reveals day's coming heat,
>   the thin, black snake divides the road into:

>   *This is what the land says now* and
>   *This is what the land says after.*

Just a few miles away history (dust before its eyes) hides
    beneath the map's pastel surface—

Sharp as a mountain's penciled bust when fog lifts,
as creek's insidious intent to tell to tell to tell.
Live oaks, redwoods, mesh of fragrant bays
shuffle in the wind, then lean in to listen,
the ink of their shade inviting.

>   *Some of the writing on the wall will be designated as truth.*

Dirt road, dust kicking up, winding toward

>   *gravel in throat,*
>   *eyes that can look beyond shade's reach*

to the glass of night,
to stories that nudge up in the dark.

What We Found Here

First light and already fog laces
the trees. Here, we stitch lives
from found remnants:

> arrowheads in limestone bedded creeks

> yellowed newspapers, and a tiny Greek statue
> left sealed into the mouth of a wall

> lip of old foundation stones that belt the soft grassed hill

> the continuous return of deer paths spelling
> across the hillside each spring.

In these truths, we find our edges: the lines of purpose that surface
even in this fog, these clouds of witness.

Trick of Sound

The hills that surround our home
have gone golden— a tenor tone
that resonates like a prayer bell
in the round bowl of the valley.

Words, carried between hills,
bend to our ears across honeyed air—

somewhere, miles away, there is a wedding.

The acoustics of this place allow the past
to rise swift as afternoon wind
and overtake today. Vows taken years before
reverberate in the thick suspended air,
valley slack as an open jaw.

The swift collage of currents
that carries the hawk's feathered body
is unmappable.

What if there are no words to carry across
just our bodies and an unknown alphabet of air?

Gift

All etymology leads to two narrow paths stubbed with grass—
one foot following the other.

There are, of course, intersections   islands
where one thought leads to another.
A gift is the act of giving, espousal, exceptional talent, poison.

And all around the seasons expel their grief and joy:
        The bright tapestries of spring stitched
        into the thawing earth, the dark, bare trees.
        The wave of summer heat ripe
        with the golden rot of decay.
        The rush of fall's airborne leaves.
        The cold wonder.

I've walked this path and passed myself
going back in the other direction,
wishing only to lift my stone tongue,
speak a word that could reach the other side.

And there have been others who have passed shaded
by trees or blurred beyond identity by tule fog.
I listen for their footsteps—
What will meet me *here* I know is meaning—

A chance to look for once at that blue dome, a few combs of clouds,
read the syntax formed by the bodies of birds:

        Light, lifting and gone.

Notes

Title page "Home-made": Quotation is from "Crusoe in England" which can be found in Elizabeth Bishop's, *The Complete Poems*.

Title page "Home-made": Quotation is from *Interviews with Tom Smith and Maria Copa: Isabel Kelly's ethnographic notes on the coast Miwok Indians of Marin and southern Sonoma counties, California; edited by Mary E.T. Collier and Sylvia Barker Thalman*.

"The Naming": Quotation is from Brothers Grimm, *The Bremen Town Musicians*.

"After Elegy": uses a combination of the following computer programming codes: XML, HTML, and Perl.

Title page "Water Root": Quotation is from Juliana Spahr's book *Well Then There Now*.

"Desire, Please Burn Off": **Arborglyphs** are tree carvings, usually of the faces of loved ones, made in the bark of aspen trees by shepherds in the High Sierras.

"At Hallig Hooge": **Hallig Hooge** is a small island off the coast of Germany. It is the second largest of the ten halligen in the Wadden Sea, and is frequently called the Queen of the Halligen. The Halligen (singular Hallig) are ten small German islands without protective dikes in the North Frisian Islands in Schleswig-Holstein. The name comes from the Celtic word *hal*, meaning "salt", a reference to the low-lying land in the region which is often flooded over with saltwater by the tides.

Title page "Mother Tree": Quotation is from Amy Lowell's Poem, "Lilacs," which can be found in *Selected Poems of Amy Lowell*.

"We Two Were Sisters of a Strange, Isolated Family": Quotation and title are from Amy Lowell's poem "Sisters," which can be found in *Selected Poems of Amy Lowell*. On the island of Leucas there are two-hundred foot white cliffs that give the island its Greek name. In antiquity the "**Leucadian Leap**" served as a trial for accused persons. If the accused survived their leap they were picked up by boat and set free. According to Ovid, the poet Sappho, desperate with love, ended her life here.

"Gold Passage": **Charlotte Mignon "Lotta" Crabtree** (1847-1924) moved from New York to Grass Valley, CA in 1853. Lola Montez, the Countess Landsfeldt, lived only a few doors away, and she began to teach the young Lotta to sing and dance. The Crabtree family moved to San Francisco in 1856, when she was nine, and by twelve she was known as "Miss Lotta, the San Francisco Favorite." She retired from the stage in 1892. **Lola Montez** (1818-1861) thrilled Gold Rush San Francisco with the "Spider Dance." In May of 1853, Lola Montez spent a year in Grass Valley, where she met Lotta Crabtree whom she mentored.

"Our Flesh, Delivered by Ghosts": **Bletting** is a process that certain fleshy fruits undergo, beyond ripening. The fruit must fall to the ground and further ripen before it is ready to eat. In fruit tree grafting, the mother tree is the tree where all grafts are tested. A **witness tree** is a tree that marks the edge or corner of a property.

Acknowledgements

Some of these poems, often in earlier versions, first appeared in the following journals and anthologies:

Bay Area Poets Coalition: "Hope" and "Sebastopol"

Boxcar Poetry Review: "Inheritance"

Calyx "Her Voice Grabbed Me So Hard I Almost Remembered Who I Was"

Certain Circuits: "The Woman at the River's Edge"

Cleveland in Prose and Poetry: "The Carp"

Eaden Water's Press Home Anthology: "What Falls from the Sky"

Fence: "Cormorant" and "A Conversation a Little Girl has with Herself is the Size of an Apple"

Hessler 2006 Poetry & Prose Annual: "The Naming"

inter|rupture: "At Hellig Hooge" and "Fear the After Thirst Diving In"

MoonLit: "We Were Two Sisters of a Strange Isolated Little Family"

Poet's Market 2013: "Photography Lesson, Point Reyes"

Raft: "Body's Code" and "Dear Real Life" and "After Elegy"

Radius: "The Distance Between" and "Our Flesh, Delivered by Ghosts"

Reed Magazine: "The Dress"

SNReview: "The View from Mercer Hospital"

Spirits: "California"

Sugarhouse Review: "Between the Word and the Sense"

Talking Writing: "Bodega Bay" and "Witness" and "Cave Redux"

The Mom Egg: "Gold Passage"

The Open Doors Poetry Zine: "A Door Poem Between the Heart and the Self"

Verse Wisconsin: "Inside/Out"

Weave: "The Gift"

Yabushka Review: "The Trick of Sound"

Zocalo: "Dinosaur"

Thank you Matt, Jackson, and Maxwell.

Thank you to my family – my parents, John and Rebecca Johnson, to my brother, Ayen Johnson, my Mother-in-law Andrea Dunkle, my Sister-in-law, Samantha Dunkle. This book is also in remembrance of my Father-in law, Dr. Kenneth Dunkle. Thank you, too, Nicole Cvitanovic for being like family.

Thank you Jane Shore and Judith Harris. Thank you to William Mathews, Sharon Olds, Jean Valentine, Melissa Hammerle, and the Golden Writers. Thank you Nicole Hefner Calihan, Ashlie Kauffman, and Melissa Peters. Thank you to Judith Oster, Mary Grimm, Gary Stonum, and Martin Helzle. Thank you to Arthur Dawson, Terry Ehret, and Judith Stone. Thank you to Squaw Valley Writers Conference faculty and staff, and David Lukas.

Thanks you, also, Phyllis Meshulam, John Johnson, Carol Lundberg, Greg Mahrer, Paula Koneazny, and Kathleen Winters. Thanks to California Poets in the Schools. Thanks to Molly Fisk and Lisa Cihlar. Thanks to my Wompo Workshop and the Napa Valley Writers Conference.

Finally, thank you to the incredible editors at Trio House Press, and to Ross Gay who have lovingly edited my work.

About the Author

Gold Passage is Iris Jamahl Dunkle's debut poetry collection. Her chapbook, *Inheritance*, was published by Finishing Line Press in 2010. Dunkle currently teaches writing and literature at Sonoma State University, Napa Valley College and with California Poets in the Schools (CPITS). She received her B.A. from the George Washington University, her M.F.A. in Poetry from New York University, and her Ph.D. in American Literature from Case Western Reserve University. She is on the staff of the Napa Valley Writers conference, and currently resides with her family in Northern California.

About the Artist

Martha Wade is a Sonoma county painter and muralist. Originally from Indiana, she grew up around artists and craftspeople. She received a BA in theatre from Oberlin College before moving to San Francisco in 1985. She worked briefly for the San Francisco Opera, and performed in local theatre productions before unintentionally beginning her career as a muralist. She saw a newspaper article about a San Francisco mural painting company, Evans and Brown, and on impulse applied for a job. She learned the nuts and bolts of the craft while working there, and was able to travel extensively, painting and installing murals both nationally and internationally.

She moved to Sonoma County in 1995 and established her own mural business, Martha Wade Design. In addition to murals, she also creates her own fine art paintings, and has recently begun branching out into graphic design. You can see her paintings at www.marthawade.com, and her murals at www.marthawadedesign.com

About the Book

Gold Passage was designed at Trio House Press through the collaboration of:

Tayve Neese, Lead Editor
Martha Wade, Cover Art: Painted Maquette
Dorinda Wegener, Cover Design
Lea Deschenes, Interior Design

The text is set in Adobe Caslon Pro.

The publication of this book is made possible, whole or in part, by the generous support of the following individuals and/or agencies:

Anonymous

About the Press

Trio House Press is a collective press. Individuals within our organization come together and are motivated by the primary shared goal of publishing distinct American voices in poetry. All THP published poets must agree to serve as Collective Members of the Trio House Press for twenty-four months after publication in order to assist with the press and bringing more Trio books into print. Award winners and published poets must serve on one of four committees: Production and Design, Distribution and Sales, Educational Development, or Fundraising and Marketing. Our Collective Members reside in cities from New York to San Francisco.

Trio House Press adheres to and supports all ethical standards and guidelines outlined by the CLMP.

The Editors of Trio House Press would like to thank Ross Gay.

CPSIA information can be obtained at www.ICGtesting.com
Printed in the USA
BVOW05s0152120316

439721BV00006B/2/P